RICKY MARTIN

A SCRAPBOOK IN WORDS AND PICTURES

by Anne M. Raso

Anne M. Raso is the editor of *Teen Girl Power* and *Kissable Pinups* for the Starlog Group and contributes to such publications as *BET Weekend* and *Sisters in Style*. She lives in New York City.

First published in the US by
Bantam Doubleday Dell BFYR
a division of
Random House, Inc.

First published in the UK by
Ebury Press, Random House,
20 Vauxhall Bridge Road,
London SW1V 2SA

Text copyright © 1999 by Anne M. Raso
Book design by Ericka Meltzer O'Rourke

Visit us on the Web!
www.randomhouse.co.uk

ISBN: 0-091-87427-0
Printed and bound in the United Kingdom at the University Press, Cambridge
10 9 8 7 6 5 4 3 2 1

Title page photographs copyright © 1999 by (top to bottom) Joy E. Scheller/London Features,
Ron Wolfson/London Features, Lawrence Marano/London Features

LATIN STYLE

Enrique Martin Morales was born on December 24, 1971, in San Juan, Puerto Rico. If you believe in the horoscope, being born under the sign of Capricorn is what gave Ricky not just ambition and perfectionism, but also profound sensitivity and powers of seduction. And even if you don't believe in the horoscope, you'd be hard-pressed to deny that Ricky has all those attributes, plus a great voice, moves, and looks. So let's take a look into the life of this handsome young man who has become a role model for pop, TV, and Broadway fans alike.

THE EARLY YEARS

At only five years old, Ricky Martin already enjoyed dancing and singing. The divorce of his parents when he was two obviously altered his life, but he knew how to keep a certain balance, and his parents always encouraged him in his ambitions. One of a large family (two younger brothers, one sister, thirty-five cousins, and twelve uncles), Ricky was a stubborn little guy, but his stubbornness is what led him to pursue his dreams.

Ricky had his initial performing experiences in school, where he acted in plays and sang in the choir. Still in his early school years, he began appearing in television commercials. Those experiences, along with singing and acting lessons, helped him lay a foundation upon which he could build to

Ricky (far right) during his years with Menudo. Copyright © 1999 by Felix/Star File

pursue his dream. And what was that dream? At the age of ten, Ricky dreamed of becoming a member of the singing group Menudo.

"I didn't want to be a singer," Ricky later confessed. "What I wanted was to be in Menudo. I wanted to give concerts, to travel, to meet pretty girls. I had been a fan of the group since it began in 1977. I was always stubbornly determined to be one of them." Ricky auditioned to join the group twice, but because of his young age, both auditions ended in rejection.

However, Ricky survived his early childhood years just fine without being a member of the singing group. He recalls, "My childhood was very healthy, near to my parents, who were divorced. I did whatever I wanted: I lived with my mother if I wanted to be with her, and with my father in the same way. I had the same affection from both of them. Although they were no longer married, they were very good friends."

MENUDO MANIA

icky's dream of becoming a member of Menudo did not die, and as fate would have it, in 1984 the group's management was looking for a replacement for the ultrapopular Ricky Melendez and hadn't yet been able to find a guy who "had it going on." When Ricky came back for his third attempt to join the group, the managers finally decided to give him the chance, and he joined the group on July 10, 1984, at the age of twelve and a half. As a member of Menudo, Ricky toured for five years at sold-out concerts all around the world. And along with other group members, he learned the value of self-discipline and the importance of his fans' devotion.

Ricky remembers the craziness of those days: "The group was mobbed—wherever they went, whether it was Philadelphia or the Philippines. We always had to stay in hotels with secret passageways like the Roosevelt in New York City—we always needed alternate routes to run out of a hotel or concert hall

if fans were chasing us. I went through quite a few changes of clothes because of girls ripping or cutting at them."

He had to move out of his family's home in Puerto Rico and into Menudo's home base in Orlando, so he was truly on his own for the first time when he joined the Fabulous Five. He has not lived in Puerto Rico since he completed his high-school education there, although he often flies down to visit family members. He remembers, "Even though we were all from Puerto Rico, our base was in Orlando. I signed the contract at eight o'clock in the morning, and at ten o'clock I was on a flight to Orlando.

"It hasn't been easy," he goes on. "All of my family lives in Puerto Rico, and I try to go there as much as I can to recharge my batteries. But I guess I'm lucky, my audience in Puerto Rico understands the reason why I needed to leave and I don't consider myself less of a Puerto Rican because I don't live in

Puerto Rico. I've learned to really appreciate who I am from a different perspective since leaving the island. I don't want to sound dramatic, but I know that's where I want to die. Puerto Rico is home."

But all good things must end. On July 10, 1989, Ricky left the group because of its strict policy that members must not be older than seventeen. He then returned to Puerto Rico to finish his school-

Ricky posing with Madonna at the Grammys.
Copyright © 1999 by Ron Wolfson/London Features

ing, after which he transplanted himself to New York for six months of rest and relaxation.

HEAD FOR THE BORDER

While in Mexico City, Ricky decided to pursue acting as well as singing. He recorded his self-titled debut solo album for Sony, and he got an offer to star in a Mexican musical called *Mama Ama El Rock 'n' Roll* (*Mom Loves the Rock 'n' Roll*). He was also cast in the popular Mexican daytime drama *Alcanzar Una Estrella II* (*To Reach a Star II*) in 1992, spending eight months as Pablo, a musician and singer in the band *Muñecos de Papel*. He even sang the theme song.

Thanks to the tremendous success of the drama, the TV band did an extensive tour in Mexico and the story was spun off into a

feature film. For his stellar performance in the film, Ricky won a Heraldo, the Mexican equivalent of the Academy Award. This helped him get a part in the short-lived American sitcom *Getting By* in 1993. At the same time, he also managed to record his second CD, *Me Amaras*.

Ricky claims he will always remember his Mexico City days with a smile: "I had a lot of friends and I was kind of adopted by this incredible family. They made it so much easier, but I got used to it easily, because I was working a lot. It was so different just being in another country—where Spanish is spoken, but it's almost another language. I will go back there anytime."

THE SOAP OPERA SHUFFLE

Ricky doing an in-store record promotion for *Vuelve*. (Copyright © 1999 by Pen/V. Zuffante/Star File)

In 1994 Ricky Martin joined the cast of ABC's *General Hospital*. With all his acting experience, he had no qualms about accepting a role on the legendary soap. This was a decisive step in his already successful career and the opportunity to present himself to a North American audience. He quickly caught the attention of the news media, which acclaimed his participation in the famous series. He played Miguel, a former pop star from Puerto Rico who fled the heartbreak of lost love and landed in Port Charles as a bartender with a mysterious past.

Naturally, the character Miguel returned to singing professionally, which gave ABC the opportunity to showcase Ricky Martin in various episodes. Most

moving scene: Miguel's ballad in tribute to his friend Stone during a hospital AIDS benefit.

When asked today whether he thinks people still associate him with Menudo or with *General Hospital,* and whether those career endeavors held him back in some way, Ricky answers, "When I left the group, I took a whole year off just to spend some time with myself. When I came back to the 'spotlight' I had a completely different image. In Latin America, they don't remember me as being with Menudo. I was a little kid in Menudo, I had long hair, and it was a different point of view; sometimes I have to remind people where

I come from. I don't mind when they ask me about the soap, I think the soap fed the music career, and the music fed the acting, like a circular process."

After dedicating two years of his career to acting, Ricky returned to his first love, music. Yes, he decided to pursue acting after he left Menudo, but since all his roles seemed to have something to do with singing and his two solo albums were doing so well, he finally realized that he was meant for music. Sony released his third album, *A Medio Vivir* (*It Means to Live*), in 1995.

Great performers and composers such as Robi Rosa (Ricky's former Menudo-mate), Ian Blake, Franco DeVita, Alejandro Sanz, Cristóbal Sansano, Mónica Naranjo, Marcos Flores, Luis Gomez Escolar, Carlos Lara, Luis Angel, Manolo Tena, and Ricky himself (in his first efforts as a songwriter) helped bring *A Medio Vivir* worldwide success. Working

under the direction of producer KC Porter (who has collaborated with artists such as Jon Bon Jovi, Boyz II Men, and Richard Marx) didn't exactly hurt the mix, either.

This third release charted not only in Latin American countries but in Europe as well. *A Medio Vivir* became a triple-platinum album, and the single "Un, Dos, Tres Maria" was double platinum in Europe alone. Ricky did concert tours around the world for more than a year, promoting his album and becoming a hit wherever he went. His songs were well received even though the lyrics were in Spanish, proving that music is indeed the universal language. Very few artists could pull this off, but then Ricky has his endless charms working for him. And fans were delighted that he was reunited with Robi, his ex-bandmate from those crazy Menudo days.

I n one of his 1996 press interviews, Ricky was asked what he'd like to do before he died and he answered, "Theater on Broadway." The executive producer of *Les Misérables* read the interview and called Ricky to audition, and he got the role of Marius, an idealistic young student revolutionary in nineteenth-century Paris. Ricky left his role on *General Hospital* and moved to the East Coast to take the Broadway job.

During his eleven-week limited engagement, Ricky won the hearts of theatergoers with his interpretation of the heartbreaking ballad "Empty Chairs at Empty Tables" as well as the moving love duet "A Heart Full of Love." He

Copyright © 1999 by Pen/V. Zuffante/Star File

reminisces fondly about the show: "I was working with incredible performers. I learned a lot from them. And my favorite scene is when Jean Valjean is going through a cathartic moment telling me his life at the end of the second act."

In 1997 Ricky was recruited to provide the singing voice of Hercules for the Spanish version of the Disney animated feature.

WORLD CUP '98

With Ricky's growing popularity around Europe and Latin America, FIFA (the World Cup's governing body) decided to contract Ricky to sing its 1998 World Cup official song, "The Cup of Life." The song is included on *Vuelve* (*It Returns*), Ricky's fourth album, released in January 1998. *Vuelve* also carries the Spanish version of Walt Disney's *Hercules* theme song, "Go the Distance," and the Spanglish version of Ricky's hit single "Un, Dos, Tres Maria."

Sony also decided in 1998 that Ricky was ready to break into the Asian market. Ricky hit that market

like a storm, going platinum, double platinum, and triple platinum in countries like Japan and Thailand.

GRAMMY GREATNESS

Ricky performed his song "La Copa de la Vida" at the forty-first annual Grammy Awards in early 1999. His performance was greeted enthusiastically by the crowd of performers in the audience. Ricky looked cool, calm, and collected as he accepted his award for Best Latin Pop Performance, wearing a gray ribbed sweater and black leather pants.

But Ricky's award nominations didn't stop at the Grammys—shortly thereafter, he was nominated for a Blockbuster Award, an Ace Award, and a World Music Award. Days after the Grammys, *Vuelve* received a large boost in sales in the United States.

HARD WORKER AND GOOD GUY

Ricky Martin is definitely on top, and his career has been marked with fun times and big breaks, but he has also worked very hard from a young age. He has even pushed himself to the point of exhaustion, and he's only beginning to reap the fruits of his labors in the United States. But Ricky has some

Ricky Martin attending an ABC event with Lilly Melgar in 1995. (Copyright © 1999 by Miranda Shen/Celebrity Photo)

key personality traits beyond his acting and singing talents that have to be mentioned.

First, Ricky really respects and admires his fans. He's got the patience of a saint when it comes to signing autographs and posing for photo ops. He even takes the time to talk to fans at length if he can. Second, Ricky's almost as passionate about helping others as he is about his own work. Although his acting and music have kept him quite busy, he gives part of his time to helping drug-addicted and abused children, and he participates in AIDS awareness campaigns. With performances in benefits such as the White Nights Festival in Russia, Disney en Las Americas AIDS Foundation, and the American Heart Association, Ricky has been able to help others and at the same time bring a bit of himself and his music to everyone.

He has performed in dozens of benefit shows and appears proud to use his celebrity to help the less fortunate. His most recent charity concert appearance was at the Tenth Annual Rainforest Benefit at New York's Carnegie Hall on April 17, 1999—British superstar Sting, who founded the event with his wife,

Trudie Styler, personally invited Ricky.

Ricky invests equal faith in hard work and a positive attitude. "Everything I've accomplished is because I've been ready for it," he says, naming Daniel Day-Lewis, Sting, and Barbra Streisand among the multifaceted performers who have inspired him. "Planning, discipline, and a good outlook are the keys to success," he adds.

And let's not forget the fact that despite a busy schedule, he always makes room to acquire

new knowledge. He concludes with a smile, "I have so much to learn! I've been in this business for twelve years, but I have a hell of a lot to learn. I have a lot to learn about myself, about realizing how great it is to be alone for a little while. Just putting my thoughts in order and finding out how to express my experiences. How to share them with the audience. I have a lot of things to talk about.

"Sometimes I don't know how, but when I sit down to write lyrics, what I want to talk about in a song . . . It is beautiful to write, to sing your own music, you know what you're talking about, you know what you're saying. The feeling that I get when I'm onstage . . . I will never change that for anything. It gives you strength, it gives you some kind of power, it gives you control. What do I want to be doing in thirty years? I want to do this; I want to do music. Let's keep studying, let's keep getting ready."

RICKY THE ROMANTIC

Ricky has always done a great job of keeping his love life under wraps, but that hasn't stopped people from guessing. He was briefly linked with Madonna in the press after they met at the 1999 Grammy Awards, and rumors flew that they would be attending the Oscars together, but that did not happen.

Despite great looks, talent, and manners that would impress your grandmother, Ricky has lost at love and claims that one never gets over a real heartbreak. He says seriously, "It's very painful. I don't think it [my heart] will ever completely heal, but you have to try to keep at least the base of who you are and believe in others and go out there and love again. I don't think you will ever get over a broken heart until you love again. No matter how hard you try to let go of that, it'll be there until you find another person to love. That's the way it's been for me."

He goes on to express his idealistic views about falling in love. "When I am in love, I give everything. It's scary when I fall in love because I

give everything. But, then again, I would never ask my girlfriend to leave her work in order to be with me—it comes with the package; it's part of it. I've been working for many years to get where I am or to where I want to be, so instead of finding someone that would be a shadow in my career, I would want to find someone that would motivate me and help me to go on and even give me ideas."

His views on romance and heartache? "I love being romantic. I love bringing a rose to a girl, and I love poems. I was in love once and we broke up and at that moment I said, 'What was I doing wrong?' That's the first thing you think when you end a relationship—'Maybe I was doing something wrong.' Then I said, 'No, I'm not going to change. I had beautiful moments in this

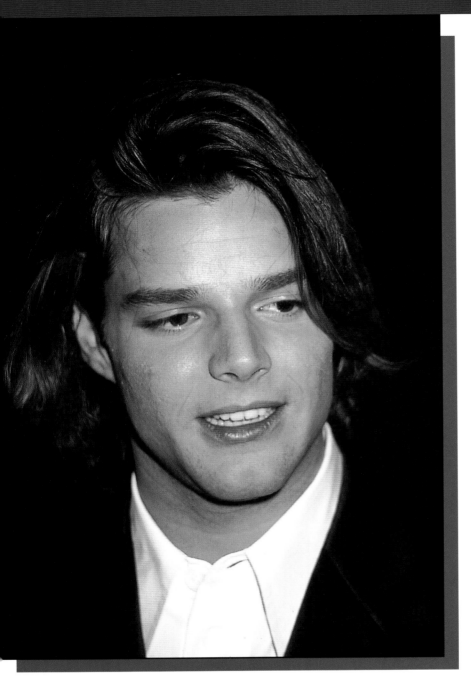

relationship and maybe those beautiful moments were because I was romantic and I read poems, and I'm not going to change.' I keep doing it, and it's just beautiful. It works for me."

Fans constantly ask Ricky the clichéd question "What's your type?" He replies candidly, "I like light-skinned Latinas, I like all Latinas. I need my culture somewhere. I need to dance to my rhythms with my partner; but then again, Cupid is stronger than any of us. If he shoots you with an arrow it doesn't matter what part of the world you're in, you will fall in love and then it's up to you to show her who you are, where you come from, and your roots. I don't close doors. Maybe I'll fall in love with a Japanese girl, you never know. But there's nothing like Latina [women]. I have to say it."

FILM, STAGE, AND TELEVISION CREDITS

Mama Ama El Rock 'n' Roll

In 1988 Ricky acted in a play titled *Mama Ama El Rock 'n' Roll* (*Mom Loves the Rock 'n' Roll*) with the great actress Angélica Vale and her daughter Angélica Maria.

Alcanzar Una Estrella II

In the late 1980s Ricky appeared in the daytime drama *Alcanzar Una Estrella II* (*To Reach a Star II*), in which he was cast with young stars such as Sacha, Bibi Gaytán, Angélica Rivera, Pedro Fernandez, and Erick Rubin. After the soap, they went on to do the film *Más Que Alcanzar Una Estrella II.*

Getting By

In September 1993 Ricky moved to California from Puerto Rico to play a part in this short-lived television comedy series.

General Hospital

From 1994 to1996, Ricky Martin was signed to play the character of Miguel Morez on the hit ABC soap opera *General Hospital.* Ricky turned in a stunning performance on the small screen and left thousands of Americans singing his praises.

Les Misérables

In June 1996 Ricky was offered his dream role on Broadway. He accepted the part of Marius in *Les Misérables*, the long-running musical based on the novel by Victor Hugo.

Hercules

Disney's thirty-fifth full-length animated feature, released in late June 1997, featured Ricky as the singing voice of the title character in the Spanish version of the film. The movie tells the classic story of Hercules, the mighty son of Zeus who lives on Earth as half man, half god. When "Herc" discovers his true origins, he sets out on a quest to prove his valor and return to Mount Olympus.

DISCOGRAPHY

Ricky Martin has recorded with the group Menudo and has been included on many compilation albums. The following is a list of his solo career albums:

Ricky Martin (C2/Sony Music/Columbia Records, 1999)

Vuelve (Sony Discos, 1998)

A Medio Vivir (Sony Discos, 1995)

Me Amaras (Sony Discos, 1993)

Ricky Martin (Sony Discos, 1991)

RICKY MARTIN: AT A GLANCE

Full name: Enrique Martin Morales
Date of birth: December 24, 1971
Zodiac sign: Capricorn
Place of birth: San Juan, Puerto Rico
Present residence: Los Angeles
Height: 6'2" (often mistakenly listed in the press as 6'1")
Weight: 165 pounds
Eye color: brown
Hair color: light brown
Parents: mother Nereida Morales, father Enrique Martin Negroni
Siblings: Fernando, Angel, Eric, Daniel, and Vanessa
Best quality: "Sincerity."
Worst quality: "Sincerity."
Fears: "Snakes and eating seafood."
The smartest thing he ever did: "Start in this business."
In his free time: "I write poems in my diary."
Underwear of choice: "I only wear white briefs—I guess I am not too original. But they do the job."
Official fan club address: Ricky Martin International Fan Club, P.O. Box 13345, Santurce Station, San Juan, PR 00908-3345